To the memory of Reg Birch – BB

The author and illustrator acknowledge with thanks the generous help
offered by the Institut du Radium in Paris, and especially Mme Gablot,
whose assistance has been invaluable.
The illustrator would also like to thank Tamsyn Barker for all her help.

This edition published 2004 by Mathew Price Limited,
The Old Glove Factory, Bristol Road, Sherborne, Dorset DT9 4HP, England

A catalogue record for this book is available from the British Library

Hardback ISBN 1-84248-121-5
Paperback ISBN 1-84248-120-7

Printed in China by Imago

BEVERLEY BIRCH

# The Search for Radium

*Marie Curie's Story*

ILLUSTRATED BY CHRISTIAN BIRMINGHAM

MATHEW PRICE LIMITED

The room was like a cave a-gleam with treasures.

Marie and Pierre Curie stood quietly together, looking. In the darkness around them, shelves and tables held the tiny glass dishes and bottles, blue-glowing, softly beautiful.

Like jewels on a dark cloth.

In that moment all tiredness, all years of struggle, all disappointments and accidents were forgotten. It was a moment of shared, silent peace.

On that icy night in the winter of 1902, in a ramshackle old shed in Paris, Marie and Pierre saw only the glow of the treasure they had conjured from the rocks and pine-needles and brown crumbling soils of a distant land.

It was like reaching the peak of a mountain Marie had been climbing for years.

She thought back to the years in Poland, as a young girl. Everything had been so hard! Teaching herself science with no teacher to guide her – just books, and more books, and her own fierce determination, and her dream that one day she would be free to study with other young people, in a university.

And always the battle to earn enough money to go to France. In Poland girls couldn't study at university. The university of Paris, in France, was the peak of Marie's dream. Six years – working, learning, saving, working, saving, learning . . . and dreaming. And then on, to a new struggle in Paris, to master French so she could understand her teachers.

Listening, thinking, reading – six more years . . .

And all that had been four years ago, before her long, painful climb up the mountain had begun. That started the day she read about the invisible rays.

She had thought X-rays were strange enough. Rays of light that you couldn't see, that went through paper, wood, metal, and – most fascinating of all – the human body, so you could take a picture of a person's bones!

A German scientist had discovered them only two years before, and now scientists everywhere were rushing to find out about them.

That's how a French scientist named Henri Becquerel had stumbled on another, different kind of ray.

A white metal called uranium, locked in a drawer, had sent out rays so powerful that they travelled right through a metal sheet and black paper. The rays had darkened a photographic film in the exact shadow-shape of the uranium.

Powerful rays, completely invisible, that no one had ever found before!

Marie was aflame with questions: what were these rays? Did other substances send them out – not just uranium? What made them happen? How strong were they?

Becquerel found that they made electricity flow through the air . . .

She pondered the problem.

. . . perhaps . . . she could measure how strong they were by measuring the electricity they caused in air? Her husband Pierre had invented just the machine – his electrometer. It could measure even the tiniest flow of electricity.

Eagerly she told Pierre her idea.

He helped her arrange the machine. When there was nothing between its two brass plates, no electricity flowed in the air and the pointer on the scale did not move.

But if something between the plates did electrify the air, the pointer *did* move. A little movement showed a small flow of electricity; a further movement showed a bigger flow; a large movement showed a very strong flow.

Marie took her first step up the mountain . . .

Quickly she collected samples of all the substances used in the school laboratories where she and Pierre worked. One at a time, she put them between the electrometer's plates and watched the scale. She tried lumps. She pounded samples to powder. She mixed, heated, cooled, wet and dried them. Each time she wrote down what she put between the plates; if the pointer moved; how far.

Suddenly she could see a pattern. It didn't matter what she did to a substance: wet, dry, hot, cold: if there was uranium in it, the pointer always moved. No uranium, no movement. And just as clear – more uranium gave stronger rays; less uranium, weaker rays!

She churned over in her mind all she knew about uranium. It is what scientists call an element, one of the basic materials (such as gold, silver, iron, carbon, oxygen and hydrogen), which make up all substances in the world. A new question was nagging at her. Did other elements besides uranium also send out Becquerel rays?

She took another step up the mountain. One by one she tested all the elements. One by one she found the answer was 'No'. That is, until she came to a grey metal called thorium. The pointer jumper high up the scale!

Her mind whirled. A hundred new questions: what about natural rocks, sand, soil? She put her thoughts to Pierre. Out came their bicycles. Off they pedalled on a new exploration . . .

Marie's room began to look like a museum. Rock and stone – rough, smooth, hard, soft; purples and pinks and greens and shining black; grains of powdery sand, gritty dirt . . .

If she was right about the elements, then she should find that only rocks, soils or sands that had uranium or thorium in them should send out the rays. Rock after rock, soil after soil went between the electrometer's brass plates.

Every single sample without thorium or uranium showed no rays.

She was right!

By now she was finding it difficult to think about the rays without a proper name for them. It was no good just calling them 'Becquerel rays' or 'uranium rays'. She wanted a new name, a word to make people imagine 'radiating rays'.

'Radioactive'. It was Marie's word. But from then on all scientists used it, and still do.

All the samples that were not radioactive Marie put to one side. Now to delve deeper into the mystery of the radioactive ones. She found an interesting lump of black rock and put it between the brass plates.

The pointer jolted.

But the rock didn't have *that* much uranium or thorium. She was puzzled.

She measured other samples of the black rock. This one moved the pointer a short way, and the next . . .

Violently the pointer jumped high.

Enormously strong rays! Much stronger than uranium or thorium could give off.

Quickly she sorted out more lumps of the black, slightly shiny rock. One was four times more radioactive that other substances with the same amount of uranium. It must be a mistake!

She did the measurements again. And then again and again. Always the same answer.

Something else must be in the rock – something much more radioactive than uranium and thorium.

But she'd already tested all the elements . . .

The idea that entered her mind then shot a thrill right through her. A new element. An unknown substance. Something never seen before.

Her growing excitement captured Pierre and he took his first step on to the mountain beside her. Something was hiding in that black rock. Something was sending out extraordinary rays. Something unknown and unseen – unless they could find it.

Their search began.

This was their plan. The shiny black rock was called pitchblende. Scientists had already worked out which of the known elements were in pitchblende. So Marie and Pierre had to separate all of these from the rock, and take them out.

Whatever was left behind must be the new element.

Their first task was to grind some pitchblende to a fine powder.

Each element needs special treatment to separate it, because each is differently built and behaves in a particular way. Some can be heated so they form a gas, like the steam in cooking. Some can be mixed with different liquids that turn the elements into hard lumps to be filtered out . . .

Each stage took time. Each stage needed endless care. They made mistakes because they were tired. Sometimes they had to try several different ways before they won: heating and mixing and filtering, mixing again, heating, filtering . . .

But they worked on from the battle with one element to the battle with the next. And when they succeeded in removing one, Pierre tested it again with the electrometer – just to be sure there were no rays. Then he tested what was left behind.

Always the pointer jolted high up the scale.

It took months to get to the hidden substance. They even chose a name for it as they worked: polonium, after Poland.

But when they finally got the polonium out, another puzzle faced them. Something was still left behind – and still immensely radioactive!

Another radioactive element, still hidden? Nothing else could explain the powerful rays.

But it was no good being sure it was there yet unable to see it –  even if Marie did name it radium, and Pierre did hope it would be beautiful. It must be in pitchblende in tiny amounts. Like one grain of sand in a bucketful! That posed a new problem. To collect enough radium to be able to see it, they needed hundreds of sacks of pitchblende – and somewhere big enough to take them all.

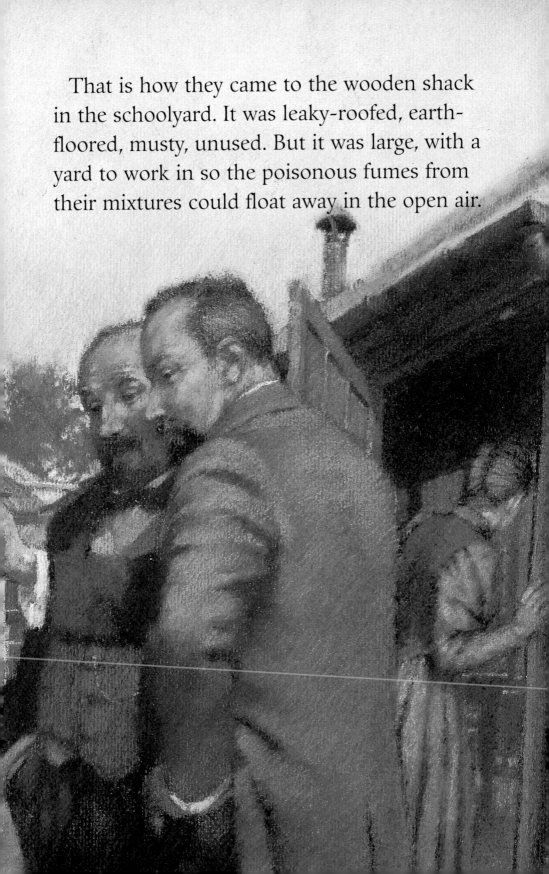

That is how they came to the wooden shack in the schoolyard. It was leaky-roofed, earth-floored, musty, unused. But it was large, with a yard to work in so the poisonous fumes from their mixtures could float away in the open air.

Some old wooden tables; furnaces, burners and pots to heat the substances; Pierre's precious electrometer – and their laboratory was ready.

But they had no pitchblende. And no money to buy any. A new mountain of effort faced them: letter after letter written to factory after factory. Someone, somewhere, they hoped, could spare enough pitchblende for their work.

Letter after letter came back carrying disappointment with it. A new round of letters, and then another, until – victory! A glass factory in Austria could give them tons of pitchblende waste.

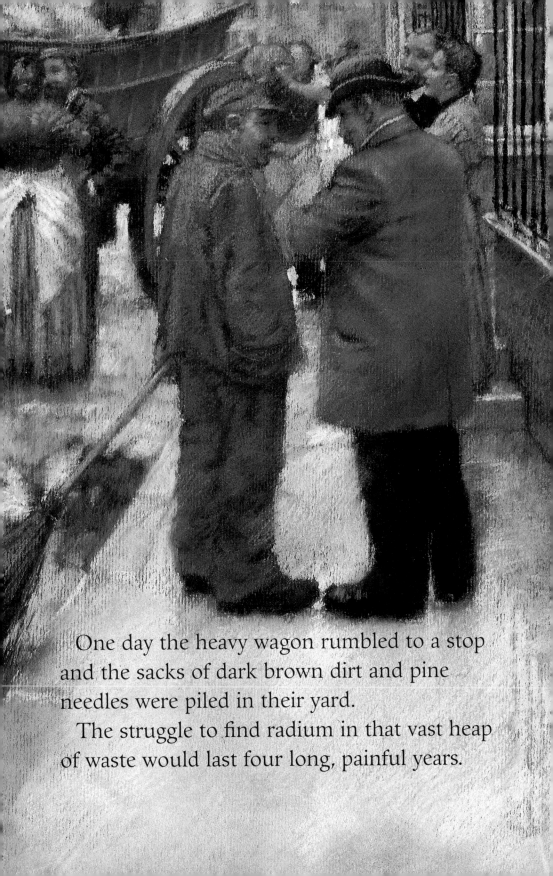

One day the heavy wagon rumbled to a stop and the sacks of dark brown dirt and pine needles were piled in their yard.

The struggle to find radium in that vast heap of waste would last four long, painful years.

First they had to take a bucketful of pitchblende, and sift it to remove the pine needles and other unwanted rubbish.

Then they ground it to a powder, put it in iron pots over a fire and added soda.

As the mixture boiled, it separated into a small amount of radioactive solid substance and a liquid that was not radioactive.

They threw away the liquid.

They took the solid substance and dissolved it in acid.

Then began the long, slow stage of mixing this new liquid with different chemicals in turn, to make each element separate.

Bucketful after bucketful went on its journey
through the sifting, mixing, heating,
dissolving, filtering . . . sackful after sackful
after sackful . . .

  Each time they took a known element out,
Pierre tested it with the electrometer.

  Then he tested what was left.

The part left behind got smaller and smaller
– until it was no more than a thimbleful that
glowed in the dark.

But its radioactivity was gigantic.

And still they hadn't seen pure radium. Still
it hid from them.

Marie lifted and carried and poured the great pots of liquid. For hours she stood over them, stirring them with a gigantic iron bar.

In the summer, the shed and yard were like one enormous furnace. The heat of the coke fires and the stench of the fumes from their scientific concoctions were suffocating, almost too much to bear.

While Marie stirred and mixed, Pierre studied the rays from their radium-rich substance. They were so powerful and gave off such an intense heat! Vastly stronger than uranium's rays – so he could find out much more clearly how they behaved, what substances they could pass through and what stopped them.

He began to realize there were at least two kinds of ray. Each behaved differently and had different strengths. And amazingly, other substances became radioactive when they were close to radium . . .

Sometimes Marie and Pierre reeled from tiredness, working to complete a difficult task long after their brains and bodies were desperate for sleep.

Strange aches and pains flowed through them, exhausting and worrying because they seemed to have no cause. Marie's fingers were cracked and sore. And the cold in winter froze them to the bone.

Sometimes the wind gusted through gaps and cracks in the shed, and blew iron and coal dust into the little dishes cradling the radium they'd plucked from the pitchblende waste.

Then, of course, they had to start again with a new bucketful, to replace it.

And sometimes they stumbled, and months of work were lost in a pile of broken china and a glowing pool on the floor . . .

Three years and nine months after she first
said that radium was in pitchblende, Marie
had a tenth of a gram of her pure new
element.

Enough to show the world. Victory!

Radium is over a million times more
radioactive than uranium, so it was a tool of
immense power. Scientists were able to use

that tool to learn that radioactivity comes from *inside* the atom: the basic building block of everything in the world. And so they began to understand the atom and the gigantic energy stored inside it.

The gateway to the nuclear age stood open. Marie Curie's tiny dish of pure radium – the labour of four long hard years – was the beginning of a vast new story with many chapters. The story is still being written today.

When Marie Curie first found polonium and radium, she was excited because they were unknown elements. But before long she and Pierre also learned that radium had important uses – it could be used to treat the disease of cancer. So Marie's discovery has saved and lengthened millions of lives.

Radium also helped Marie to develop some important scientific ideas. Scientists then knew that elements were made up of building blocks called atoms – but they thought that atoms were the smallest possible pieces of matter. They did not think atoms could be broken down into anything smaller. But Marie wondered if radioactivity was going on inside the atoms. Perhaps there were even tinier pieces, called particles, which moved about inside the atom? Later, other scientists explored that idea, using the power of her radium. They gained new understandings of the atom, and the enormous energy which was locked inside it: nuclear energy. Our nuclear age depends on those understandings.

As years went by, scientists found many more ways of using radioactive substances. Now, radioactivity is used to run nuclear power stations and nuclear submarines; to check the thickness and quality of paper and metal in industry; to find how plants use the fertilizers they are given; to trace pollution in rivers; to test concrete under oceans; to measure the oil flow in pipelines; and to sterilize hospital equipment.

Radium made the Curies very ill. Marie Curie died from her contact with it. Now we know that radiation causes cancerous diseases, and people who work with any radioactive materials must protect themselves with clothes and equipment which stops rays from harming them.

## MARIE CURIE
### 1867-1934

Marie Curie was the first woman in Europe to become a Doctor of Science. At the time, people believed that women could not understand science as well as men, nor work as hard. Marie proved that she was not only as clever and hard-working, but she was also one of the best scientists in the world. So her story has inspired many girls, and it is now common for women to become scientists – and to be very good at it.

# The Science Stories Books
## by Beverley Birch

Benjamin Franklin's Adventures with Electricity
*Illustrated by Robin Bell Corfield*

Marconi's Battle for Radio
*Illustrated by Robin Bell Corfield*

Marie Curie's Search for Radium
*Illustrated by Christian Birmingham*

Pasteur's Fight against Microbes
*Illustrated by Christian Birmingham*